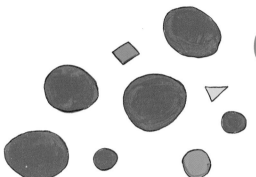

Play-Doh Art Projects

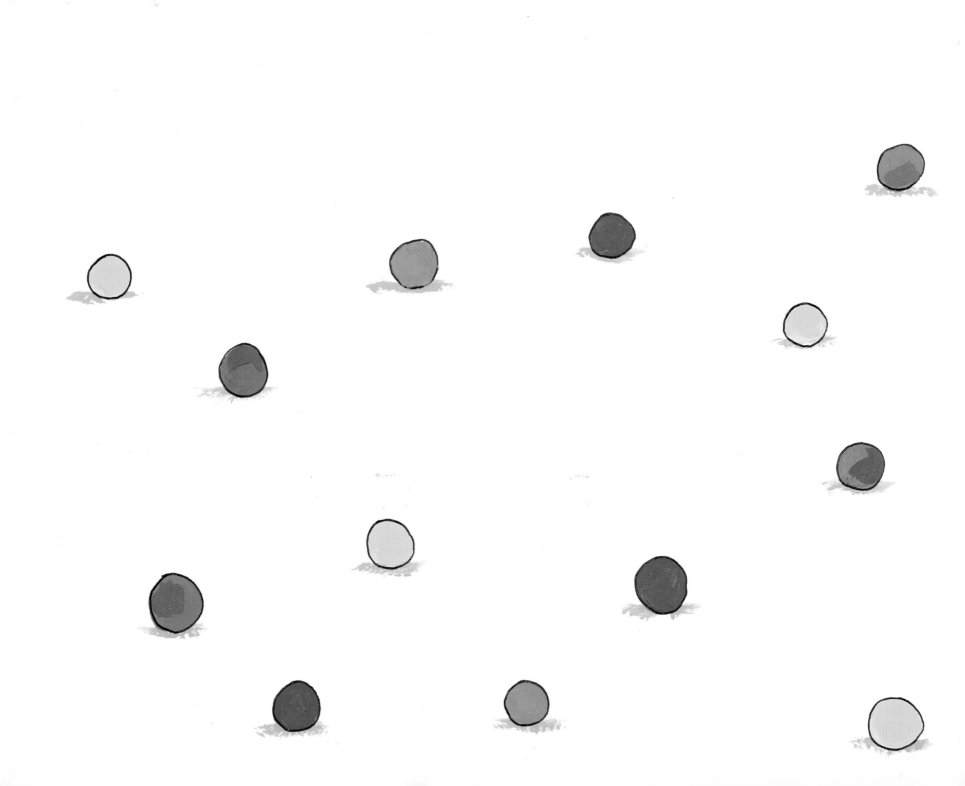

ART PROJECTS

BY KATHY ROSS

Illustrated by Sharon Hawkins Vargo

The Millbrook Press   Brookfield, Connecticut

For Joe, Laura, Kyle, and Jamie—kr

To my (EHS) high school art teacher, Mr. Larry Acciani,
for great art projects—sv

Copyright © 2002 by Kathy Ross
Illustrations © 2002 by Sharon Vargo
Play-Doh is a registered trademark of Hasbro identifying its quality
modeling compound, and is used with permission of Hasbro, Inc.,
Pawtucket, RI.

Published by The Millbrook Press, Inc.
2 Old New Milford Road, Brookfield, Connecticut 06804
www.millbrookpress.com

Printed in Hong Kong
5 4 3 2 1 (lib. bdg.)
5 4 3 2 1 (trade)

Library of Congress Cataloging-in-Publication Data
Ross, Kathy (Katharine Reynolds), 1948-
Play-doh art projects / by Kathy Ross ; illustrated by Sharon Hawkins Vargo.
p. cm.
ISBN: 0-7613-2267-1 (lib. bdg.) – ISBN 0-7613-1481-4 (trade)
1. Art—Technique—Juvenile literature. 2. Design—Technique—Juvenile literature.
3. Polymer clay craft—Juvenile literature. 4. Clay modeling—Juvenile literature. [1. Clay
modeling. 2. Handicraft.] I. Title: Art projects. II. Vargo, Sharon Hawkins, ill. III. Title.
N7430 .R66 2001   745.5—dc21   00-066826

Contents

Mixing Colors 6

Introduction 7

Play-Doh Mosaic 8

Fabergé Egg 10

Play-Doh Pointillism 12

Play-Doh Etching 14

Sculpting on the Go 16

Play-Doh Relief 18

Play-Doh Weaving 20

Play-Doh China Design 22

Embellished Plate 24

Designer Stationery 26

Automotive Design with Play-Doh 28

Hairstyles with Play-Doh 30

Play-Doh Makeup 32

Play-Doh Jewelry 34

Play-Doh Cake Decorating 36

Box of Play-Doh Candy 38

Play-Doh Fashions 40

Decorated Play-Doh Hat 42

Play-Doh Designer Necktie 44

Play-Doh Designer Sneaker 46

Mixing Colors

Play-Doh modeling compound artists can work with their own color pallette, just like a painter. To create more colors for your crafts, gradually add small amounts of darker Play-Doh to lighter Play-Doh and knead until blended.

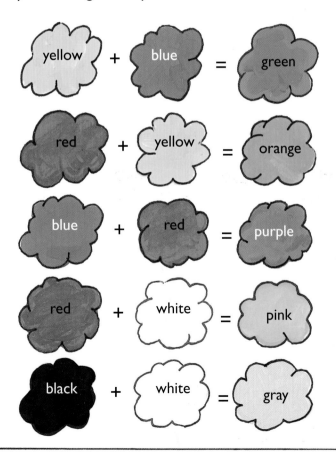

yellow + blue = green

red + yellow = orange

blue + red = purple

red + white = pink

black + white = gray

Introduction

When you think of using your artistic skills to play with Play-Doh modeling compound, sculpting is the first thing that comes to mind. There is something very satisfying about squeezing and modeling and shaping the colorful material into whatever your imagination can conjure up and your skill will allow.

This book offers ways for all kinds of budding artists to hone their knowledge and skills with Play-Doh. The projects here will introduce you to the world of art and design. Using Play-Doh and a few simple household items, you can try your hand at automotive design, cake decorating, or fashion design. You can make a picture out of dots in the style of Pointillism. You can create a mosaic or an etching. Hats, jewelry, and even a wild-looking sneaker are all in the realm of the Play-Doh designer.

The projects in this book are made with just five Play-Doh colors: red, green, blue, yellow, and brown. Don't let my choices limit your creativity. YOU are the artist, so make the projects in the colors that please you.

If you love Play-Doh as much as I do, you are really going to have fun with this book!

Kathy Ross

A mosaic is a picture made of different colored pieces of material arranged to create a design, scene, or figure.

Here is what you need:

safety scissors

Play-Doh Mosaic

Here is what you do:

1. Flatten out a small ball of each color of Play-Doh.

2. Cut the Play-Doh into 1-inch (2.5-cm) pieces of various shapes, to look like shards of broken china. You can cut them into even tinier pieces if you want to make a more detailed mosaic design.

shallow, clear, plastic disposable container with lid

Play-Doh modeling compound in a variety of colors

aluminum foil

3. Arrange the pieces in the bottom of the plastic container to create a mosaic picture.

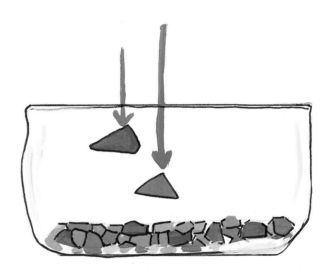

To save your mosaic picture to display for a while, cover the picture with a piece of aluminum foil or cellophane. Crumple more foil to place on top of the picture to hold it firmly in place when you snap the lid on the container. Stand the container up so that the picture is visible through the bottom of the container. If you chose a round container you will need to lean it against something to keep it from rolling.

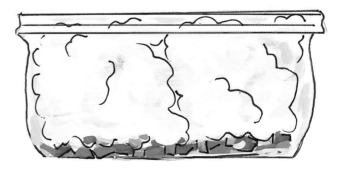

9

Fabergé eggs are highly decorated egg shapes covered in rich colors and jewels.

Here is what you need:

Play-Doh modeling compound in colors of your choice

Fabergé Egg

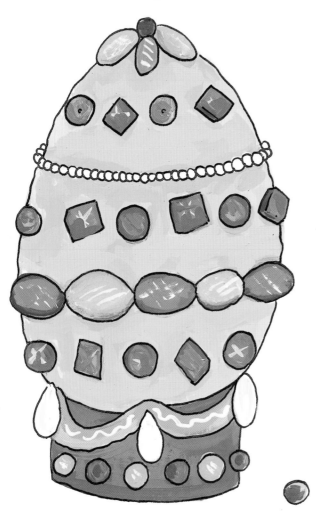

Here is what you do:

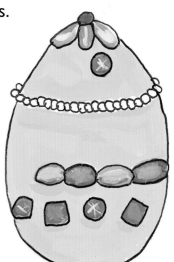

1. Mold the Play-Doh into an egg shape.

2. Make "jewels" out of Play-Doh colors of your choice. You can wrap little balls of Play-Doh around a string to look like beads.

3. Decorate the egg by pressing the Play-Doh jewels into the Play-Doh egg in a pretty design.

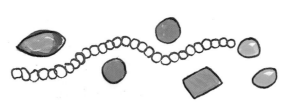

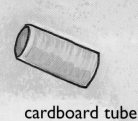
cardboard tube

construction paper
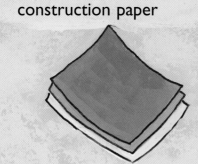

safety
scissors

white glue

4. Make a stand for the egg by cutting a 1-inch (2.5cm) ring from the end of the cardboard tube.

5. Cover the ring with construction paper. You can glue jewels on the egg holder, too, if you wish.

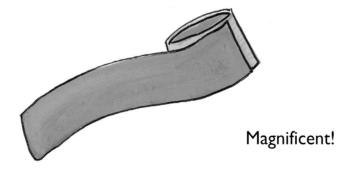

Magnificent!

Using tiny dots to make a picture is called pointillism.

Play-Doh Pointillism

Here is what you need:

hole punch

Here is what you do:

1. Use the pencil to sketch a small, simple picture on the tray.

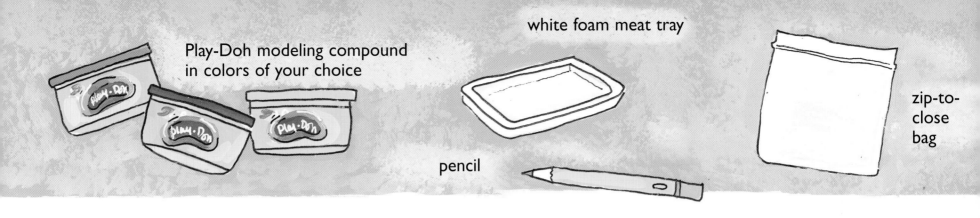

Play-Doh modeling compound in colors of your choice

white foam meat tray

zip-to-close bag

pencil

2. Use your hand to flatten out a piece of Play-Doh. Make it thin enough to fit easily into the hole punch. Repeat with each color.

3. With the hole punch, punch out lots of dots in the different colors.

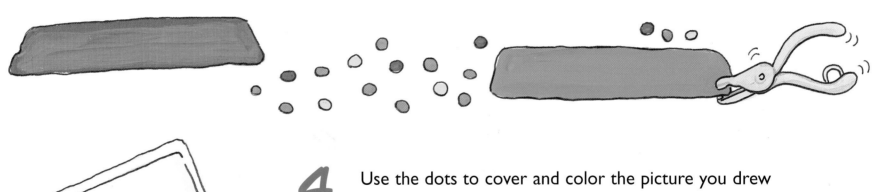

4. Use the dots to cover and color the picture you drew on the tray.

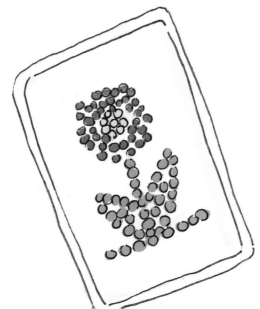

That's it! A picture all made of dots!

If you want to save the picture to display for a while, slip it into a zip-to-close bag.

13

An etching is made by scratching a picture into a surface.

Play-Doh Etching

square lid from a disposable plastic container

Here is what you do:

1. Cover a 4- by 4-inch (10- by 10-cm) square in the center of the lid with flattened splotches of Play-Doh in various bright colors. Make the colored layer as thin as you can.

2. Flatten out a piece of dark Play-Doh until it is large enough to cover the colored square of Play-Doh. Make the dark layer as thin as you can.

Play-Doh modeling compound in one dark color and various bright colors of your choice

zip-to-close bag

pencil

3. Set the dark Play-Doh gently over the colored Play-Doh.

4. Use the pencil to trim the edges off the dark Play-Doh so that it exactly covers the colored Play-Doh square underneath

5. Use the pencil to mark a simple shape in the dark layer of Play-Doh.

6. Carefully pick out the dark shape to expose the colorful layer underneath.

If you want to save the Play-Doh etching for a while, display the project in a zip-to-close bag.

A sculpture is a three-dimensional work of art.

Here is what you need:

Play-Doh modeling compound

Sculpting on the Go

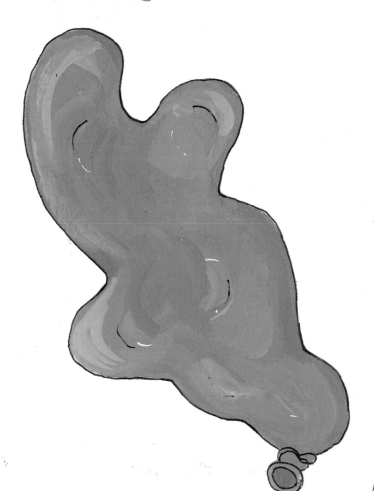

Here is what you do:

1. Push as much Play-Doh as you can down into the balloon. It is a big help to have someone hold the neck of the balloon stretched open for you.

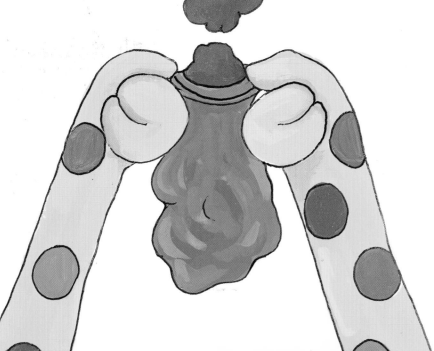

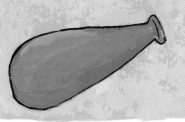

9-inch (23-cm)
round balloon

zip-to-close bag

2. When the balloon is full, but not stretched, tie the neck of the balloon in a knot.

3. Shape the Play-Doh filled balloon into different artistic creations.

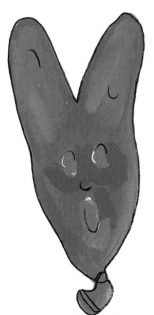

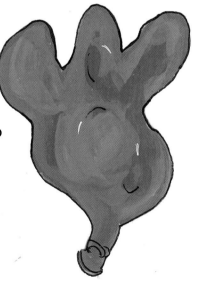

This is a great item to tuck in your pocket to use when you have a few minutes with nothing to do.

Storing the sculpting balloon in a zip-to-close bag when it is not being used will help it to stay fresh and pliable longer.

17

A relief is a picture made with layers of art material to give a three-dimensional look.

Here is what you need:

3- to 4-inch
(8- to 10-cm)
plastic lid

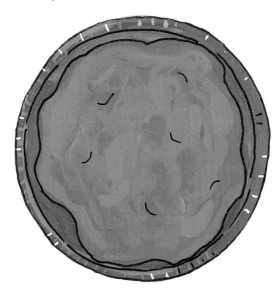

Play-Doh Relief

Here is what you do:

1. Decide what kind of picture you want to make. Cover the inside of the lid with a thin layer of Play-Doh for the background of the picture.

small ink stamps

Play-Doh modeling compound in colors of your choice

safety scissors

clear packing tape

2. Use the ink stamps to imprint pictures in different colors of Play-Doh. Cut the pictures out to use as part of the Play-Doh scene. Arrange them on the background.

Cover the Play-Doh relief in clear packing tape if you want to save it to display for a while.

3. Shape simple details from Play-Doh to add to the picture.

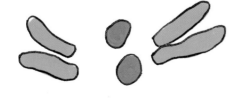

19

Play-Doh Weaving

Here is what you do:

1. Roll out pieces of Play-Doh to create long, thin strips.

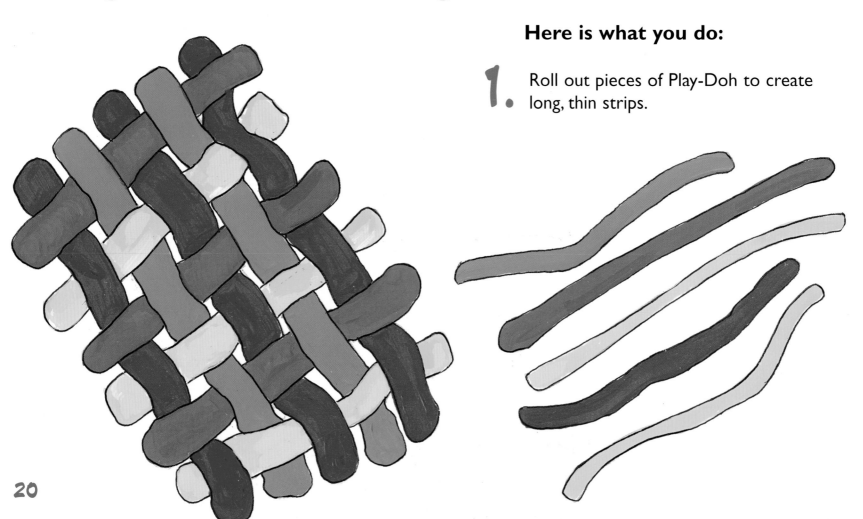

20

 Play-Doh modeling compound in two or more colors of your choice

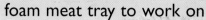 foam meat tray to work on

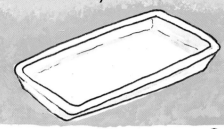

2. Lay down four or more strips next to each other across the Styrofoam tray.

3. Carefully weave other Play-Doh strips over and under the first ones to create a pattern.

4. When you have woven strips all the way across the ones placed on the tray, gently press the strips together to secure them.

5. Pick up the woven Play-Doh and trim the ends of the strips to make them even.

Varying the Play-Doh colors and using different combinations of colors will create very different results in the pattern.
Try it!

Designing china patterns is fun.

white foam plate

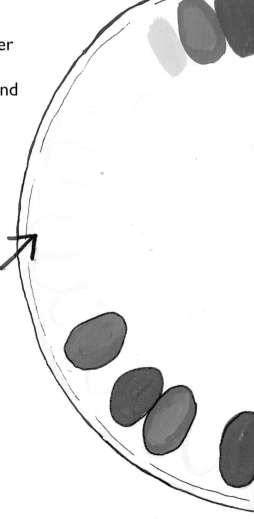

Play-Doh China Design

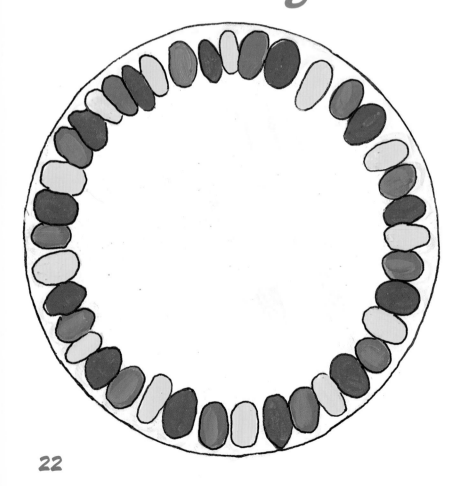

Here is what you do:

1. Notice how real dinner plates have a design stamped around the edge and sometimes a design or picture in the middle. Use the Play-Doh to press a design of your own onto the plate, or to enhance a border design that's already there.

22

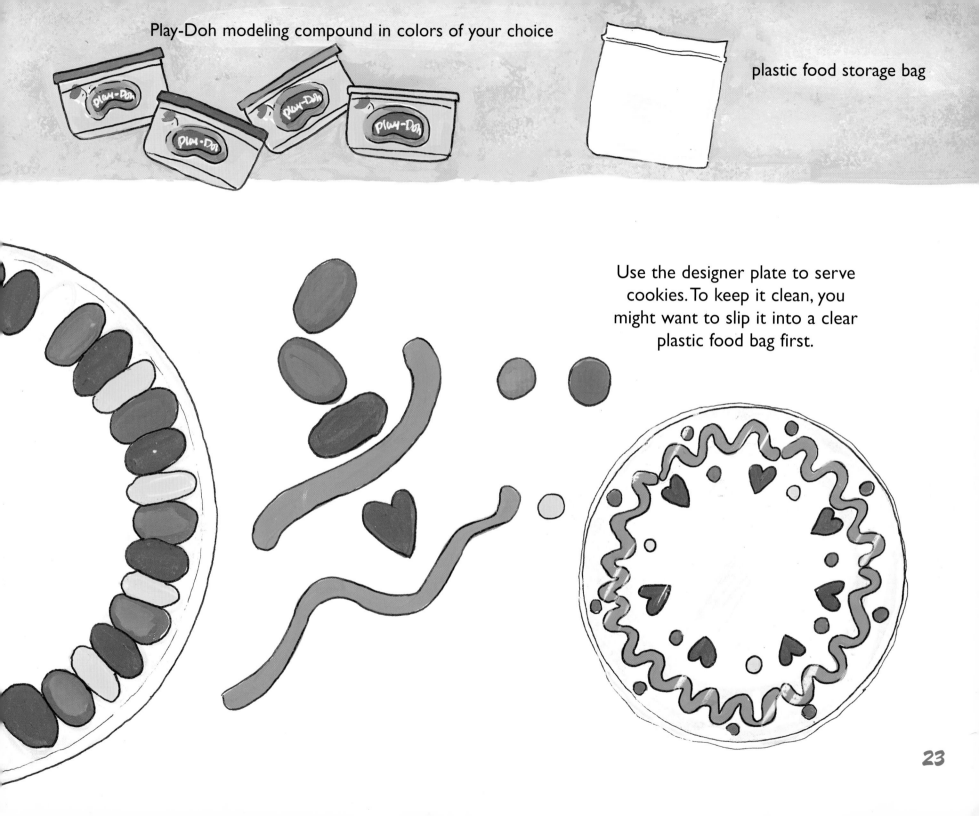

Play-Doh modeling compound in colors of your choice

plastic food storage bag

Use the designer plate to serve cookies. To keep it clean, you might want to slip it into a clear plastic food bag first.

You can also use Play-Doh to embellish a preprinted paper plate.

Here is what you need:

paper plate with holiday or party picture printed on it

Embellished Plate

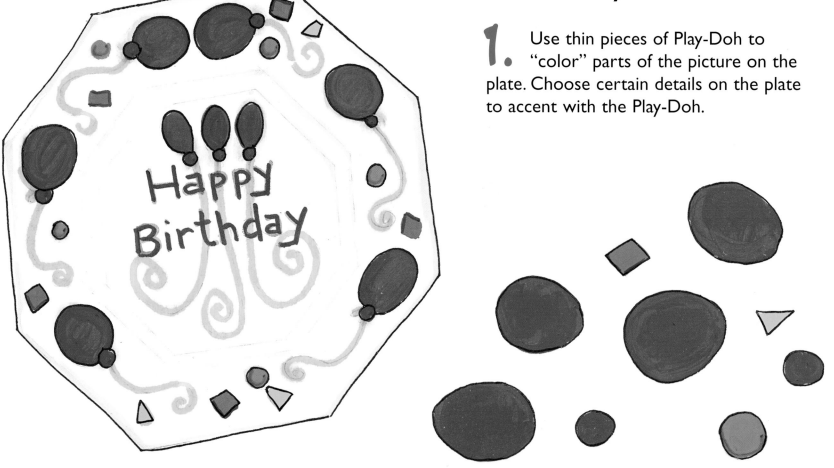

Here is what you do:

1. Use thin pieces of Play-Doh to "color" parts of the picture on the plate. Choose certain details on the plate to accent with the Play-Doh.

Play-Doh modeling compound in colors of your choice

plastic food storage bag

2. Slip the plate into a clear plastic food bag to use it. Clean the plate by changing the plastic bag.

Happy Birthday

Happy Birthday

Play-Doh plates make an unusual addition to a holiday table.

Play-Doh is just what the young artist needs to create designer stationery.

Designer Stationery

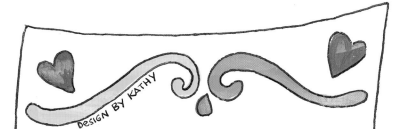

Dear Grandma,
How are you? I am fine. I designed this stationery with Play-Doh.
We are visiting you next weekend. See you soon!
Love, Kathy

Here is what you need:

blank writing paper

Here is what you do:

1. Because you will need most of the space on the paper for writing, you should only decorate the paper at the corners and/or along the edges.

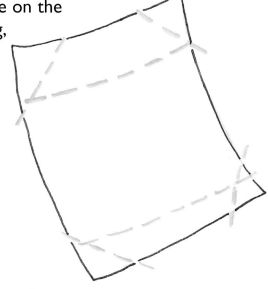

2. Make tiny shapes or figures from the Play-Doh. Make them as flat as you can.

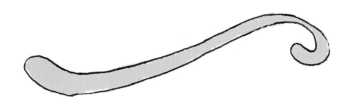

 envelopes to fit
the paper

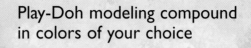 Play-Doh modeling compound
in colors of your choice

clear packing tape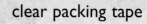

safety scissors

3. Set the figures or shapes where you want them on the
writing paper.

4. Cover the figures with clear packing tape. Trim off any edges
of the tape that stick out over the edge of the paper.

Play-Doh stationery would make a
very nice gift. Be sure to sign your
work by writing in tiny letters
somewhere on the paper "Design
by" and write your name.

Have you ever thought about designing a car? Try this project.

small plastic or
metal toy car

Automotive Design with Play-Doh

Here is what you do:

1. Decide what color you would like the car to be. Cover the outside top of the toy car with a thin layer of that color Play-Doh. Make sure the Play-Doh does not interfere with the working of the wheels.

Play-Doh modeling compound in all colors

2. Use different colors of Play-Doh to add details to the car, such as lights, doors, and racing stripes. You are the designer, so you get to decide what the car needs.

Design two or more Play-Doh cars. Have a demolition derby on a washable floor or table to see which design holds up the best.

Here's how to create new hairstyles for your doll friends.

Hairstyles with Play-Doh

Here is what you need:

plastic doll

Here is what you do:

1. Create strands of hair by squeezing Play-Doh through the garlic press.

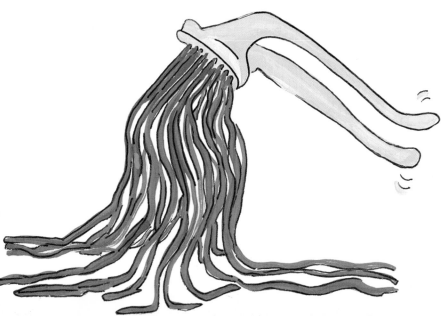

30

Play-Doh modeling compound in
colors of your choice

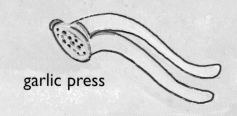

garlic press

2. Arrange the Play-Doh strands on the head of the doll to create a hairstyle.

3. Add ribbons, barrettes, or other hair jewelry made from different colors of Play-Doh.

Try lots of different
hair colors and styles
on the doll.

31

Use Play-Doh to be a makeup artist.

Here is what you need:

plastic doll

Play-Doh Makeup

Here is what you do:

1. Decide what kind of face you would like to give the doll. (A clown face is an easy one to start with.)

Play-Doh modeling compound in colors of your choice

2. Shape the makeup from different colors of Play-Doh and press it on the face of the doll.

You can give the doll some makeup, or create a new face. How about the face of a favorite animal?

Play-Doh jewelry makes great gifts for your friends.

Play-Doh modeling compound

Play-Doh Jewelry

Here is what you do:

1. Flatten out the Play-Doh on a smooth, washable surface.

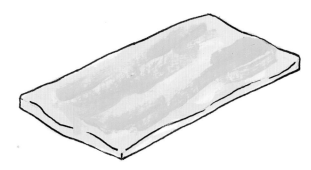

2. Use an ink stamp to stamp a picture on the Play-Doh.

34

clean ink stamps

safety
scissors

sticky-back
pinback

3. Carefully pick up the Play-Doh. Trim away the extra Play-Doh around the picture.

4. Let the Play-Doh air-dry for several days.

5. When it is hard, press a sticky-back pinback on the back of the picture and wear it as a pin.

You can use one of the larger ink stamps that are actually a little scene, and use markers to color the scene once the Play-Doh is dry. This is best done on a light color or white Play-Doh so that the marker colors show up.

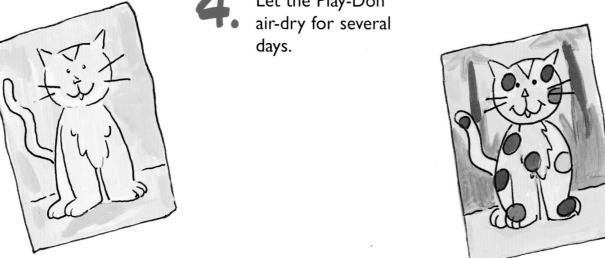

Try using your artistic talents
to decorate a cake.

Here is what you need:

plastic lid from
a spray can

Play-Doh Cake Decorating

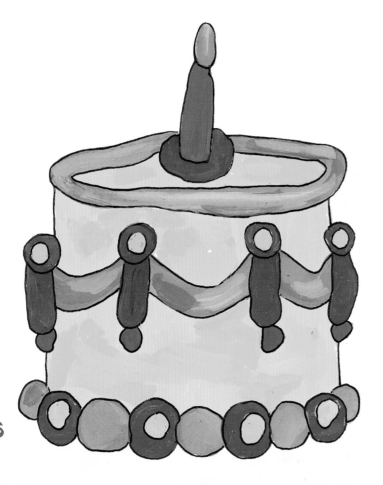

Here is what you do:

1. Cover the outside of the plastic lid
with Play-Doh to "frost" it to look like
a little cake.

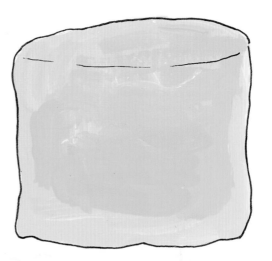

Play-Doh modeling compound in colors of your choice

zip-to-close bag

2. Use contrasting colors of Play-Doh to make decorations for the cake.

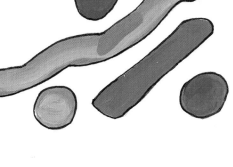

This cake is perfect to use when throwing a birthday party for one of your doll friends. Store it in a zip-to-close bag to keep it fresh until the big day.

Wouldn't it be fun to design candy!

small, empty candy box

Box of Play-Doh Candy

Here is what you do:

1. Shape different colors of Play-Doh into candy balls to fit in each wrapper.

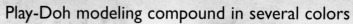

2. Use bits of Play-Doh in contrasting colors to decorate each candy in a different way.

Does your candy look good enough to eat? Well, *don't* do it!

Try your hand at fashion design!

plastic doll

Play-Doh Fashions

Here is what you do:

1. Use the Play-Doh to actually dress your doll friend. Start with the body of the doll. Mold the Play-Doh around the doll to create a dress or shirt and pants. Add details to the clothes using Play-Doh in contrasting colors.

40

Play-Doh modeling compound in a variety of colors

2. Create shoes for the doll by molding Play-Doh around the feet.

3. Finally, shape Play-Doh over the top of the doll head to create a hat. Decorate the hat with contrasting bits of Play-Doh.

You might want to decorate the Play-Doh fashions using ribbons, or lace or other decorative items.

Make some hilarious hats!

Decorated Play-Doh Hat

plastic disposable bowl

Here is what you do:

1. Turn the plastic bowl over to look like a hat.

Play-Doh modeling compound in a variety of colors

2. Use the Play-Doh to shape a hatband and other decorations for the hat.

Make several different hats and have your doll and stuffed animal friends put on a hat show.

43

Try your hand at designing a necktie.

Play-Doh Designer Necktie

Here is what you need:

old necktie, the plainer the better

Here is what you do:

1. Cut off the wide end of the necktie so that it just fits in the zip-to-close bag.

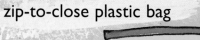 zip-to-close plastic bag

Play-Doh modeling compound in colors of your choice

safety scissors

stapler

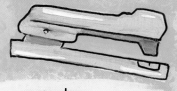

2. Put the cut tie end in the bag.

3. Staple the top of the tie to the back of the bag to hold it in place.

4. Close the bag.

5. Use pieces of Play-Doh to create designs on the plastic bag over the necktie.

Go wild! Designing neckties is a very creative job!

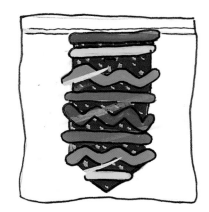

45

Would you like to work as a designer for a sneaker company? Start practicing.

old sneaker

Play-Doh Designer Sneaker

Here is what you do:

1. Run an old sneaker through the washing machine to clean it. Dry it completely.

2. If you wish, you or an adult can spray-paint the old sneaker to give it a uniform work surface. This looks nice, but is not essential to the project.

46

Play-Doh modeling compound in colors of your choice

spray paint

DAILY NEWS

newspaper

3. Use bits of Play-Doh to create your own design on the sneaker.

4. When you're finished admiring your sneaker, remove the design and wipe the sneaker with a damp cloth. This will leave it all ready for sneaker designing on another day.

Would you really wear sneakers decorated like that?

About the Author and Artist

During her thirty years as a teacher and director of nursery school programs in upstate New York, Kathy Ross has used a *lot* of Play Doh modeling compound! She is the author of more than thirty-five craft books for young children, among them The Holiday Crafts for Kids series, and *Crafts for All Seasons, Crafts from Your Favorite Fairy Tales, Christmas Crafts to Give as Gifts*, and *Crafts from Your Favorite Children's Songs.*

A graduate of Pratt Institute, Sharon Vargo lives near Indianapolis with her husband and four teenage sons. Ms. Vargo is the author/illustrator of *Señor Felipe's Alphabet Adventure*, and the illustrator of another Kathy Ross book, *Make Yourself a Monster.*

Kathy and Sharon have collaborated on another Play-Doh craft book, *Play-Doh Animal Fun.*